December '71

To dear Beth,

In sincere appreciation
of "everything" that you
have been to us and
all that you are ....

Lyd & Torts

A Mother Is Love

A MOTHER IS LOVE

Beautiful Writings
In Tribute to Mothers

Selected by

Mary Dawson Hughes

Illustrated by

Muriel Wood

HALLMARK EDITIONS

Contents

The Meaning of Motherhood
5

A Mother's Children Are Her Jewels
21

Famous Mothers and Children
33

When the Children Are Grown
49

The Meaning of Motherhood

'*UTTER CONFIDENCE AND LOVE*'
In his autobiography Promise at Dawn, *Romain Gary tells of being given a tennis racquet, as a child, and then being unable to play tennis because the courts at the Imperial Park Club required a steep membership fee. His mother was determined that her son would* not *be denied those courts, fee or no fee:*

Seeing that lack of money made it impossible for me to enter the Parc Impérial, my mother became righteously indignant. The matter, she announced, would not rest at that. She stubbed out her cigarette in a saucer, grabbed her cloak and her cane, and ordered me to fetch my racquet and to follow her that very instant to the Club du Parc Impérial. There, the club secretary was summoned, and, since my mother had a very carrying voice, he lost no time in obeying, followed by the club president, who rejoiced in the admirable name of Garibaldi and who also answered the call at full speed. My mother, standing in the middle of the room, with her hat slightly askew, and

5

brandishing her cane, let them know exactly what she thought of them. What! With a little practice I might become a champion of France and defend my country's flag against foreigners, but no, because of some trivial and vulgar matter of money, I was forbidden to go onto the courts! All she was prepared to say to these gentlemen at this time was that they had not the interests of their country at heart, and this she would proclaim at the top of her voice, as the mother of a Frenchman—I was not yet naturalized but that, obviously, was a minor matter—and she insisted on my being admitted to the Club courts, there and then. . . .

"Madame," [Garibaldi] said, "I must ask you to moderate your voice. His Majesty King Gustav of Sweden is sitting only a few steps from here, and I beg you not to make a scandal."

His words had on my mother an almost magical effect. A smile, at once naive and radiant with wonder, which I knew only too well, showed on her face and she rushed forward.

An old gentleman was taking tea on the lawn under a white parasol. He was wearing white flannel trousers, a blue and black blazer and a straw "boater" slightly tilted over one ear. King Gustav V was a frequent visitor to the Riviera and its tennis courts. His celebrated straw hat appeared regularly on the front page of the local papers.

My mother did not hesitate for a moment. She made a deep curtsy and then, pointing her stick at the president and secretary of the club, exclaimed: "I crave justice of Your Majesty! My young son, who will soon be fourteen, has a quite extraordinary gift for lawn tennis and these bad Frenchmen are making it impossible for him to practice here. The whole of our fortune has been seized by the Bolsheviks and we are unable to pay the subscription. I come to Your Majesty for help and protection. . . ."

His Majesty Gustav V was, at that time, already a very old man and this, combined no doubt with Swedish phlegm, accounted for the fact that he seemed not in the least surprised. He took the cigar from his lips, gave my mother a solemn look and me a casual glance and, turning to his coach: "Hit a few up with him," he said, "and let's see how he does."

My mother's face brightened. The fact that I was completely inexperienced as a tennis player didn't worry her in the least. She had confidence in me. She knew who I was. She knew that I had it in me. The trivial day-to-day details of life, the little practical considerations didn't count for her. For a second I hesitated, then, at sight of that expression of utter confidence and love, I swallowed my shame and my fear, sighed deeply, lowered my head and went forth to my execution.

It was a quick business, but it sometimes seems to me that I am still on that court. Needless to say, I did my best. I jumped, dived, bounced, pirouetted, ran, fell, bounced up again, flew through the air, clanging and spinning like a disjointed marionette, but the most I can say is that I did, just once, touch the ball, and then only on the wood of my racquet—and all this under the imperturbable gaze of the King of Sweden, who watched me coldly from under his famous straw hat....

When the coach at last took pity on me, and I went back to the lawn, . . . the King of Sweden saved us and the guests from a scene that would be too awful even to try to imagine. The old gentleman touched his straw hat and with infinite courtesy and kindliness—though it used to be reported that he was not an easy man to get on with— said: "I think that these gentlemen will agree with me: we have just witnessed something quite admirable . . . Monsieur Garibaldi"—and I remember that the word "Monsieur" had a more than usually sepulchral sound on his lips—"I will pay this young man's subscription: he has shown both courage and determination."

Ever since then I have loved Sweden. But I never again set foot in the Parc Impérial.

'WE CANNOT MEASURE LOVE'

In this moving selection, actress Deborah Kerr describes her feelings on the day when her four-year-old daughter discovered the full meaning of numbers—and turning to her mother, said, "Mummy, I love you ten times":

My daughter Francesca was about four years old when she first became aware that numbers were not just new words in her vocabulary or names of digits, but that they can be useful to express quantity. This step, as all parents learn, follows the "so big" stage.

One memorable day, Francesca turned to me to express her love with the help of her new-found knowledge and said, "Mummy, I love you ten times," followed by deep thought and "I love you twenty times."

After another short pause, she reached a breathless pinnacle with "I love you six hundred times."

A grateful hug and kiss from me produced a tiny frown and more concentrated thought which disappeared in a sigh of relief in her final outburst, "Mummy, I love you outside the line of the numbers."

My child's words touched me so deeply that I have never forgotten a moment of that scene, or the wisdom of her sudden discovery that you cannot measure love!

The insight that children "discover" never ceases to amaze me. Somehow their minds, uncluttered by the tensions of responsibility, can reach directly into the heart of a problem and make it brilliantly clear.

A knowledge that love is immeasurable is actually very subtle. And yet my four-year-old understood it completely, without the mechanics of logic—with only the instinct of the young. That day, that moment, my daughter knew what adults so often forget: we can neither demand nor give a love that can be counted or measured. We cannot measure love—and should not. But we can accept it, cherish it, nurture it, and thank the Lord for it.

'THE PARABLE OF THE
TWO MOTHERS'

The Biblical parable of two mothers who claimed the same child, in I Kings 3:16-27, *is a tribute to a mother's feelings for her child:*

Then two [women] came to the king, and stood before him. The one woman said, "Oh, my lord, this woman and I dwell in the same house; and I gave birth to a child while she was in the house. Then on the third day after I was delivered, this woman also gave birth; and we were alone; there was no one else with us in the house, only we two were in the house. And this woman's son died in the night, because she lay on it. And she arose at midnight, and took my son from beside me, while your maidservant slept, and laid it in her bosom, and laid her dead child in my bosom. When I rose in the morning to nurse my child, behold, it was dead; but when I looked at it closely in the morning, behold, it was not the child that I had borne." But the other woman said, "No, the living child is mine, and the dead child is yours." The first said, "No, the dead child is yours, and the living child is mine." Thus they spoke before the king.

Then the king said, "The one says, 'This is my son that is alive, and your son is dead'; and the other says, 'No; but your son is dead, and my son is the living one.'" And the king said, "Bring me a sword." So a sword was brought before the king. And the king said, "Divide the living child in two, and give half to the one, and half to the other." Then the woman whose son was alive said to the king, because her heart yearned for her son, "Oh, my lord, give her the living child, and by no means slay it." But the other said, "It shall be neither mine nor yours; divide it." Then the king answered and said, "Give the living child to the first woman, and by no means slay it; she is its mother."

'I BOILED EVERYTHING BUT THE BABY'

In the true story of her life with a rare and unforgettable religious leader, A Man Called Peter, *Catherine Marshall gives us a record of love, faith, and courage that has been an inspiration to millions. In this selection from her book, she recalls the early months of motherhood:*

I turned out to be one of those disgustingly conscientious modern mothers who sterilizes every article in sight, boiling everything but the baby. After Peter John's advent, not only were the days of easy housework gone, but also all easygoing vacation trips. I thought that this lone child had to have a ton of equipment even for a brief holiday. It always took us at least three hours of hard work to load the car for any trip.

First came innumerable suitcases, then a collapsible baby buggy, a folding play pen, a bathinette, a baby seat for the car, and a sterilizer for bottles. At first quite patient, Peter would grow more and more exasperated as I continued to trot out load after load. "Catherine, where in th' thunder do you think I'm going to put all this stuff? One baby couldn't possibly use *all that*. This car is *not* a truck." But he would roll up his sleeves, shove and heave, carry and figure and shift, with beads of perspiration standing out on his forehead, until finally, somehow, everything was in the car. . . .

Finally, I would come out, with a toidy-seat in a laundry bag flung over one shoulder, a Sterno stove with cans of baby food—assorted spinach, peas, and prunes—in one hand, juggling with the other Peter John Marshall himself. Then wedged in between boxes, bundles, and suitcases, Peter would drive off, muttering that he really did not think a few days away from the office was worth all this, and that this car might not be a truck, but it surely drove like one today. The trunk of the car would be so loaded it was scarcely off the ground.

By the time we reached the outskirts of town, I had already begun to wonder whether I had remembered to leave a note for the milkman, to stop the evening paper, and to put down the bedroom windows. . . .

I had read too many books on child care and sanitation; I was germ-conscious. Hence the aforementioned laundry bag also contained a bottle of Lysol solution and clean rags. Wherever we were going for a holiday, our path across the United States was marked by a string of filling-station rest rooms which I had sanitized for the benefit of our baby.

Peter, a man of about average patience, had to learn to wait and wait—and wait. He would stand outside, chaperoning the car, always hopeful that surely the baby and I couldn't take *much* longer. He hoped that I would emerge from the mysterious depths of the ladies' room with the gleam of triumph in my eyes. If the gleam were missing, he knew we would have to stop at another filling station thirty miles down the road. Those poor creatures who have not gone through this period with a child really have no chance to learn patience.

An ounce of mother is worth a pound of clergy.
—Spanish proverb

14

'MY HEART STARTED SINGING'
The most popular motion picture of all time, "The
Sound of Music," *was based on the autobiography
of Maria Augusta Trapp,* The Story of the Trapp
Family Singers. *In this selection from her book,
the mother of ten describes the arrival of the
youngest member of the famous family:*

Oh, time and again [I was told] that one *had to
have* a doctor and one *had* to go to a hospital to
have a baby. I was finally persuaded to make one
concession: the doctor. But go to a hospital—that
was ridiculous. Why? What for? I wasn't sick. In
Europe you went to a hospital when you were
dangerously sick, and many people died there, but
babies were born at home. Would they in the hospital allow my husband to sit at my bedside? Could
I hold his hand, look into his eyes? Could my family be in the next room, singing and praying? The
answer to all these questions was "no."

All right, that settled it. I tried to explain that a
baby had to be born *into* a home, received by loving hands, not into a hospital, surrounded by
ghostly looking doctors and masked nurses, into
the atmosphere of sterilizers and antiseptics.
That's why I would ask the doctor to come to our
house.

But I had to find the doctor first. I tried many,

but each time I mentioned the word "at home," they didn't want to take the case.

When I was very tired and discouraged, I found a young doctor in our neighborhood, young and a little nervous about the whole idea, but he said he would come.

I consoled him.

"Don't worry. There is nothing wrong, I know all about it. It is the most natural thing in the world. You just have to sit in the next room, and I'll call you when I need you."

His eyes widened, and he opened his mouth to speak, but closed it again in utter amazement.

And so it happened. The evening came when I knew it was time. Everything went the old way. The family gathered in the living room, reciting the rosary aloud. Then they sang hymns. Then they prayed again. The doors were open, and I could hear them. Georg was there next to me, and his good, firm hands patted me once in a while, as he repeated: "Soon she will be here, our Barbara," and then we both smiled. The doctor had not come yet.

Then it had to be: "Call him now and tell him to be quick."

When he arrived, he looked troubled. He had a nurse with him––a sweet-looking young girl. They were washing their hands when all of a sudden I had to squeeze Georg's hand very hard, and time seemed to stand still. Then I heard a funny little squeak. The doctor, pale, beads of perspiration on his forehead, turned to me and said—I couldn't understand what—and then carried something in his right hand through the room. It was all over. At that minute a full chorale downstairs started: "Now thank we all our God!"

The doctor, in the middle of the room, turned around.

"What's that?" he gasped.

And then I saw what he was holding: my precious baby—head down!

My heart almost stopped. I was sure he would drop her.

"Watch out—don't break her!" I cried.

"Her! Why—it's a boy!" he said reproachfully.

What? I must have misunderstood. Georg bent over me.

"Barbara is a boy," he smiled.

My heart started singing: "Now thank we all our God!"

A mother is not a person to lean on, but a person to make leaning unnecessary.

—Dorothy Canfield Fisher

'TWO KINDS OF FEELING'

Margaret Mead, a great anthropologist and humanitarian, describes in her book Family *the universal feelings of a mother for her child. Her words reveal the depth of understanding and wisdom acquired over 40 years of study:*

Often, as a mother bathes, feeds, and dresses her child, her face expresses two kinds of feeling that seem contradictory to the child and to the bystander. There is the look of unconditional devotion and blind pride in this, her child, and at the same time a look of anxious appraisal as she holds the infant away from her breast or watches the toddler's first stumbling steps and rocking gait.

For the child must go forth from the warmth and safety of its mother's care—first to take a few steps across the room, then to join playmates, and later to go to school, to work, to experience courtship and marriage, and to establish a new home. A boy must learn how different he is from his mother; he must learn that his life is turned outward to the world. A girl must learn, as she walks beside her mother, that she is both like her mother and a person in her own right. It is one of the basic complications of a mother's life that she must teach one thing to her sons and other things to her daughters.

Some peoples emphasize the mother's task more than the child's; they say that it is the mother, not the child, who is weaned. But all peoples, however differently they phrase the mystery of conception and provide for the care and safety of the mother and the child at birth, make provision—some well and others in a blundering way—for this double aspect of motherhood. All peoples build into their conception of the relationship of mother and child the care that must continue and the slowly awakening recognition that these are two persons—at birth, at physical weaning, at the child's first step, and at the child's first word that allows the child to call from a distance. And as the child lets go of its mother's hand, [it is] sure that it can return to be fed and rocked and comforted. . . .

On this unbroken continuity, on this ebb and flow of feeling between the child and the mothering woman, depends the child's sense of being a whole, continuing person—the same person today, yesterday, and tomorrow, the same person tired or rested, hungry or satiated, sleepy or wakeful, adventurous or quietly contented.

All that I am, my mother made me.
                                        —John Quincy Adams

A Mother's Children
Are Her Jewels

'*TURNING THE TABLES*'
Helen Hayes, in her autobiography On Reflection, *describes with humor and insight a particularly trying day during the early years of her "work-worn motherhood." As she recalls it:*

Jamie enraged and enchanted and eventually exhausted the rest of us. . . . When [we] had Bunty Cobb MacNaughton's little boy Charles stay with us during the London Blitz, he and Jamie became minikin and manikin, monkey see, monkey do. They were inseparable. They were ganging up on the dogs, the servants, and me. Too infrequently would they go at each other, a most welcome sight.

One day, the two kids were particularly obnoxious to one of the dogs, and I, in despair, remembered something my sister-in-law Helen Bishop had told me. When she was small and the children in the house were being naughty, her mother used to gather them to her knee and say, "I have been a terrible mother. If I were a good mother, you would all be good children and wouldn't be doing all these terrible things. I've been so bad as a mother that I want you to punish me."

She would then direct her plea to the ringleader.

"Hit me, Darling. No, I mean it. I deserve to be hit."

Her loving children would start whimpering, "No, no, Mother, please, we'll be good. We're *sorry*!" When she forced one of them to give her a token slap, a great wail would go up and all the imps would cling to their mother, begging for forgiveness. After they had comforted her and she them, they would go off, red-eyed and chastened.

I was absolutely touched by this charming cure; it was so creative. Jamie was racing around like an Indian, smacking [our dog] Turvey's bottom with a stick. It was in the midst of their cookie feud.

"Jamie!" I beckoned. "Come here, Darling."

He and his little partner in crime cautiously approached me. I was at the pool, sitting in a low beach chair in my bathing suit.

"Don't be afraid, Jamie. I want to talk to you."

The boys stood at my side as I rested my book on my lap.

I repeated the Georgianna MacArthur dialogue, ending sanctimoniously with "If you must hit someone, hit me, your wicked mother, not poor Turvey!"

Jamie pulled his ear to make sure he had heard correctly. His eyes were round with disbelief. What he usually heard was the maternal, "If you do not leave that poor animal alone, I will kick you to kingdom come."

This was all strange to Jamie—a brand-new mom. Our English house guest had all the innocence of the Artful Dodger.

"Hit her, Jamie," he encouraged my son. "Go on and hit her."

I could have slapped him.

"Yes, I deserve it, Jamie. I've been a bad mother."

It was beautiful: Jamie was rendered utterly helpless. He just stared at me.

"She told you to hit her," young MacNaughton pressed on. "Go ahead and hit her."

Jamie was roused from his reverie. He turned to his friend and then to me. I felt like Mae Marsh in *Over the Hill*—all cameo, lace dickey, and work-worn-motherhood. My son picked up the stick with which he had been harassing Turvey, took a low swing, and cracked me across the shins with all his might. . . .

I could never catch him. It was [his father] who got the chance to use the hairbrush.

'MY MOTHER IS BEAUTIFUL'

What makes a mother beautiful? The way her children see her, suggests author Wallace Irwin in this selection. Here the author, "Houdini," is faced with unusual competition at camp between little "Scuttle" and littler "Strawberry":

One night Scuttle comes to me, looking pretty down. "Houdini," he said, "I guess I made Strawberry sore. Gee. He's dumb to be sore."

I was used to the kids telling me a little of everything, so I asked, "Why's he sore?"

"We got to talking about mothers."

"That shouldn't start a war," I said.

"But Strawberry got sore. I didn't say a thing

about *his* mother, and he couldn't say much. He said she wasn't all wet, but she wasn't anything to advertise. And he said, 'You think everything you've got's beautiful. Your crawl-stroke and your mother and everything.'"

I gave Scuttle a lecture on being high-hat. Boys shouldn't be high-hat. Boasting makes enemies, gets you nowhere. I talked very fine, but it was the way Scuttle looked at me—I knew he hadn't said it all. There was something I couldn't fool with, like religious conviction.

"Is she really very beautiful?" I asked.

"Yes, sir." You could watch his eyes and be convinced.

"In what way?"

"Houdini, I guess you know when a woman's beautiful. It's just the way her face looks." This was no description, and Leonardo da Vinci couldn't have given a better one. This boy knew his mother was beautiful, and he couldn't tell why. . . .

I tried to be sore at Scuttle; but when I saw him at night in the Main House, pegging away with his red fountain pen, just talking to his mother with ink on paper, I knew that what he'd said amounted to more than kid show-off.

Well, the season was over after a while. On the last day of camp we always have a shindig with speeches and ice cream and a presentation of medals. This pleases the parents when they come to take the boys home. Scuttle, the night before the big racket, was proud as a peacock—he'd won the gold medal for swimming, his beautiful mother would be there to see it pinned on. Strawberry was booked for a second prize. Poor Strawberry. Second in swimming, second in mothers. . . .

The ceremony was set for noon, and droves of parents motored in. Kissing and reunions all over the lot. I was busy, but my eye was out for Scuttle's mother. . . .

[I saw Strawberry's mother first]. . . . She was ravingly angelic to the eye. All violet—eyes, hair, gown—that's how she looked. Slim and young and used to being gazed at. Glorious!

I saw the two boys coming up the trail. Scuttle was running, eager as a pup. Strawberry was hanging back. I just had to see what Scuttle would do when he could meet his idol face to face. . . .

I saw him jump into the crowd like a little wild dog, let out a whoop and grab a shortish, fattish lady around the neck. "Mother, I got the gold medal," he yelled, "and I want you to sit on the front seat."

Her clothes were a sort of washed-out gray, like her eyes. She had a tired face, rather made-up. Her hair was bleached, but she had a nice mouth, just as Scuttle had told me.

When Strawberry saw the perfect woman in violet he said, "Hello, Mother." I suppose she kissed him. She was mainly worried about his necktie, and what sort of effect she was making.

Scuttle and the homely one were walking arm in arm. They hadn't an ounce of good looks between them, but they were tremendously beautiful, as I saw them. It proved what he had said about his mother—it's just the way her face looks.

'THESE ARE MY JEWELS'

Through the ages, a treasure-trove of folklore has accumulated describing the feats and feelings of mothers—some mythical, some actual. One famous tale was recorded in the first century A.D. by the Roman statesman and philosopher, Seneca:

There once was a Roman lady well adorned with jewels who called on Cornelia, the mother of two boys who afterwards became influential and famous. . . .

The visitor, noticing that Cornelia had no jewels on her person, asked, "Where are your jewels?"

Cornelia sent for the two little boys and said, "These are my jewels."

These four words are among the most famous words ever spoken.

'MOTHER KNOWS BEST'

What mother has never doubted her competence as a mother? In her warm book Special Delivery, *author Shirley Jackson captures this universal reaction with a touch of humor:*

Sooner or later you are going to be left alone with this baby. All alone, just you and Baby and an all-pervading panic.

You are reasonably sure by now that you are not going to sit down on him, or put the diaper on over his head, but by golly, that is just about all you *are* sure of. . . .

There is the crib you set up so lovingly for Baby, you and his father, telling one another delightedly that Baby would lie *here*, and his little clothes would be put in *there*, and we can hear him if he makes the slightest noise at night. (Hear him? Get three blocks away and see if you can hear him make the slightest noise at night) and *here* is where he'll have his bath, and *here* . . . well, here is Baby. . . .

And what is he doing, this baby, rich in infinite knowledge, full of beauty and wonder and delight, perfect and small and most incredible of all— alive and individual? You know what he is doing.

He is making a racket altogether out of proportion to his size and strength. The nurses in the hospital knew what to do when he yelled like that. In the hospital they could *always* do something. He never yelled like this before. There must be something they forgot to tell you, some vital fact they all assumed you would know, some perfectly natural thing to do when Baby cries. . . . Everyone else knows what to to when a baby cries and there is something lacking in your makeup and you had no right to have children at all and the doctor should have told you instead of letting you go ahead and what will your mother say when she finds out you are some kind of a monster instead of a normal mother and maybe if you called the hospital and asked them nicely they would take him back. . . . No, he won't stop. But go ahead and call your doctor anyway, if you want to. You won't be able to hear anything over the phone, of course, but you will have the reassuring feeling that there is some other human being in the world besides you and this noise machine.

Don't bother to call your husband. He will only tell you that gosh, maybe there's something wrong with the kid, and you better call the doctor. When you say you've just *called* the doctor he will say well, maybe you better call the doctor again. After you have talked to your husband you can always call your mother. If she is a sensible grandmother —and grandmothers are almost always eminently sensible in this respect—she will have to hang up because she is laughing her head off. This is no comfort. . . .

Doubts about being fit to raise a child are best settled before the child is old enough to bring them up himself. . . . The truly farsighted baby is the one who learns in his cradle that his mother is going to wonder endlessly about her shortcomings as a parent, and who never allows her to stop wondering for a minute. Prepare your defense: assume from the very first minute that Mother *does* know best, that no week-old child can dictate to *you*, that your own solid common sense and proverbial intelligence are enough to carry you through, that from this very minute on, you are never going to reverse a decision once made, and whatever you say, agreeable or not, is going to be final.

Let me know how you come out.

'WHAT IS A MOTHER?'

What is a mother? Two enterprising reporters, Joan Scobey and Lee Parr McGrath, decided to ask the experts—children. In their book, What Is a Mother, *they report:*

A mother is the only one, if she sings your favorite song, it stops thundering. —Louise

Mothers are wonderful! She spends all her time on you. A mother is just like God, except God is better. —Laura

It is lucky that we have a mother because if we did not have a mother everything would be in a big big mess. —Fred

What is a mother? When I have something to tell somebody I can tell my mother sometimes but not all the times. —Betsy

A mother is a person too. —David

Famous Mothers and Children

'HER TENDERNESS AND HIDDEN GRACE'

Marie Curie, co-discoverer of radium and winner of the Nobel Prize, is remembered by her daughter Eve as a devoted mother—not a world-famed scientist. In her tender biography of her mother, titled Madame Curie, *Eve recalls how her mother tried to instill in both her daughters an independence of spirit and strength of character to protect them from insensitive curiosity-seekers:*

The creature who wanted us to be invulnerable was herself too tender, too delicate, too much gifted for suffering. She, who had voluntarily accustomed us to be undemonstrative, would no doubt have wished, without confessing it, to have us embrace and cajole her more. She, who wanted us to be insensitive, shriveled with grief at the least sign of indifference. Never did she put our "insensibility" to the test by chastizing us for our pranks. The traditional punishments, from a harmless box on the ear to "standing in the corner" or being deprived of pudding, were unknown at home. Unknown, too, were cries and scenes: my mother would not allow anybody to raise his voice, whether in anger or in joy. One day when [my sister] Irène had been impertinent, she wanted to "make an example" and decided not to speak to her for two days. These hours were a painful trial for her and for Irène—but, of the two of them, the more punished was Marie: unsettled, wandering miserably about the mournful house, she suffered more than her daughter.

Like a great many children, we were probably selfish and inattentive to shades of feeling. Just the same we perceived the charm, the restrained tenderness and the hidden grace of her [whom] we called—in the first line of our letters spotted with ink, stupid little letters which, tied up with confectioners' ribbons, Marie kept until her death— "Darling Mé," "My sweet darling," "My sweet," or else, most often, "Sweet Mé."

Sweet, too sweet "Mé," who could hardly be heard, who spoke to us almost timidly, who wanted to be neither feared nor respected nor admired. . . . Sweet Mé who, along the years, neglected completely to apprise us that she was not a mother like every other mother, not a professor crushed under daily tasks, but an exceptional human being, an illustrious woman.

'A MOTHER'S FAITH'

Thomas Edison, the inventor of the light bulb, phonograph, motion pictures, and many other innovations that changed man's world, credits his mother with his success:

I did not have my mother very long, but in that length of time she cast over me an influence which has lasted all my life. . . . If it had not been for her appreciation and her faith in me at a critical time in my experience, I should very likely never have become an inventor.

A MOTHER'S "HEALTHY WARNING"

Actress Lilli Palmer, reminiscing about her mother in "I Say What I Think," recalls how her mother gave her the courage to be herself:

My mother was born on the river Rhine, where people are gay and easygoing, where they drink much wine and don't care who likes them. When I was a child I often heard from her a healthy warning, especially when I came crying that someone didn't like me and demanding to know what I could do to make him or her like me.

"Everybody's friend is everybody's fool," she would say serenely; or sometimes, "Many enemies mean much honor," or "Where there's much sun there's much shadow."

I have interpreted those ideas in my own way. I don't set out to antagonize people, or to be aggressive or provocative, but I have never made a special concession just for the purpose of being liked. I've spoken my mind even when I knew that what I said might be unpopular, because I believe that to speak your mind is essential, to take part in a controversy is important. It has never been my nature to sit back and keep quiet for fear of treading on somebody's toes.

The danger of being too sensitive to what others think is strongly illustrated in the play *Death of a Salesman*. The author makes an important cause of the demoralization of his hero the fact that he cared too much whether he was well liked. He was afraid ever to make an enemy, and this hastened his destruction.

My mother made me immune to that fear in early youth. You can't go through life only making friends, I realized very soon.

If, for a good cause, you must make an enemy, accept the fact. As long as your conscience is clear, you will find that you have strengthened not only your determination but your character.

'OUR GLORIOUS LIFE WITH OUR CHILDREN'

Nobel Prize-winning author Pearl Buck describes in her book My Several Worlds *the deep love and faith that prompted her to seek the responsibility of adopting nine children:*

For me a house without children cannot be a home. I do not know why the people who love children are so often prevented by accident from having them, but, God be thanked, there are many who have children and leave them, for one reason or another, and then others can take them for love's sake. . . .

When the house, then, was finished in its first stage, the rose garden planted, a small swimming pool dug under the shade of the big black walnut tree, we approached our one adopted child, then eleven years old, and asked her what she thought of our adopting two little boys as soon as possible, and then a year or so later, a girl and a boy. She reflected for some weeks and then months, and we gave her plenty of time, and when she felt adjusted to her new home, she decided that it would be "nice" to have babies. The three of us then proceeded to an excellent adoptive agency and made ourselves known and began the process necessary to prove ourselves good parents and a "nice" family. It did not take too long in those days, the process was courteous and civilized, and in due course the big third-floor bedroom became a nursery, but without a nurse, for we wanted to take care of the two lively babies ourselves. A year and a half later they were joined by a small but equally lively boy and girl, each a few weeks old.

That was eighteen years ago. The four of them are now in late adolescence and are all but over the last even of that. In the rich years between the day they came home and today . . . we have had a glorious life with our children, making plenty of mistakes with them, I am sure, and losing patience on a grand scale occasionally, and they with us, but we have had a glorious time nevertheless, and thank God for every minute of it.

'NO BETTER FRIEND'

Eleanor Roosevelt describes, in her Autobiography, *the long and arduous road to understanding with her daughter Anna—and the rich rewards they enjoyed when the road-blocks were overcome. In this selection, Anna is 15 and has just entered a private girls' school in New York; her father, Franklin Delano Roosevelt, has recently suffered his first crippling attack of paralysis:*

I did not realize how set and rigid New York schools were and that a girl coming in from outside would be looked upon by all the children as an outsider and would hardly be noticed by the teachers. Anna was very unhappy, though I did not realize it. She felt lost, and the different methods of teaching bewildered her. She tried to hide her feelings by being rather devil-may-care about her marks and her association with the other girls. . . .

The situation grew in her mind to a point where she felt that I did not care for her and was not giving her any consideration. . . . There were times at the dinner table when she would annoy her father so much that he would be severe with her and a scene would ensue, then she would burst into tears and go sobbing to her room. . . .

I realize now that my attitude toward her had been wrong. She was an adolescent girl and I still treated her like a child and thought of her as a child. It never occurred to me to take her into my confidence and consult with her about our difficulties or tell her just what her father was going through in getting his nerves back into condition.

I have always had a bad tendency to shut up like a clam, particularly when things are going badly; and that attitude was accentuated, I think, as regards my children. I had done so much for them and planned everything and managed everything, as far as the household was concerned, for so many years that it never occurred to me that the time comes, particularly with a girl, when it is important to make her your confidante. If I had realized this I might have saved Anna and myself several years of real unhappiness. I would have understood her a great deal better because she would have been able to talk to me freely, and she would have understood me and probably understood her father and all he was fighting against.

As it was, I am responsible for having given her a most unhappy time, and we can both be extremely grateful for the fact that finally the entire situation got on my nerves and one afternoon in the spring, when I was trying to read to the two youngest boys, I suddenly found myself sobbing as I read. I could not think why I was sobbing, nor could I stop. . . . The two little boys went off to bed and I sat on the sofa in the sitting room and sobbed and sobbed. I could not go to dinner in this condition. Finally I found an empty room in my mother-in-law's house, as she had moved to the country. I locked the door and poured cold water on a towel and mopped my face. Eventually I pulled myself together, for it requires an audience, as a rule, to keep on these emotional jags. This is the one and only time I remember in my entire life having gone to pieces in this particular manner. From that time on I seemed to have got rid of nerves and uncontrollable tears, for never again has either of them bothered me.

The effect, however, was rather good on Anna, because she began to straighten out, and at last she poured out some of her troubles and told me she had been wrong and she knew that I loved her and from that day to this our mutual understanding has constantly improved.

Today no one could ask for a better friend than I have in Anna or she has in me. Perhaps because it grew slowly, the bond between us is all the stronger. No one can tell either of us anything about the other; and though we may not always think alike or act alike, we always respect each other's motives, and there is a type of sympathetic understanding between us which would make a real misunderstanding quite impossible.

'A HEART SO LARGE'

Mark Twain credits his mother, who was an invalid for most of her 88 years, with a compassion and "persuasive eloquence" that affected him deeply as a boy and young man. In this selection from his Autobiography, *Twain describes his mother and then recalls an incident that captures the essence of what she instilled in her son:*

Technically speaking, she had no career; but she had a character and it was of a fine and striking and lovable sort. . . .

She had a slender, small body but a large heart —a heart so large that everybody's grief and everybody's joys found welcome in it and hospitable accommodation. The greatest difference which I find between her and the rest of the people whom I have known is this, and it is a remarkable one: those others felt a strong interest in a few things, whereas to the very day of her death she felt a strong interest in the whole world and everything and everybody in it. In all her life she never knew such a thing as a half-hearted interest in affairs and people, or an interest which drew a line and left out certain affairs and was indifferent to certain people. The invalid who takes a strenuous and indestructible interest in everything and everybody but himself, and to whom a dull moment is an unknown thing and an impossibility, is a formidable adversary for disease and a hard invalid to vanquish. I am certain that it was this feature of my mother's make-up that carried her so far toward ninety.

Her interest in people and other animals was warm, personal, friendly. She always found something to excuse, and as a rule to love, in the toughest of them—even if she had to put it there herself. She was the natural ally and friend of the friendless. . . .

When her pity or her indignation was stirred by hurt or shame inflicted upon some defenseless person or creature, she was the most eloquent person I have heard speak. It was seldom eloquence of a fiery or violent sort, but gentle, pitying, persuasive, appealing; and so genuine and nobly and simply worded and so touchingly uttered, that many times I have seen it win the reluctant and splendid applause of tears. Whenever anybody or any creature was being oppressed, the fears that belonged to her sex and her small stature retired to the rear and her soldierly qualities came promptly to the front. One day in our village I saw a vicious devil of a Corsican, a common terror in the town, chasing his grown daughter past cautious male citizens with a heavy rope in his hand and declaring he would wear it out on her. My mother spread her door wide to the refugee and then, instead of closing and locking it after her, stood in it and stretched her arms across it, barring the way. The man swore, cursed, threatened her with his rope; but she did not flinch or show any sign of fear; she only stood straight and fine and lashed him, shamed him, derided him, defied him in tones not audible to the middle of the street but audible to the man's conscience and dormant manhood; and he asked her pardon and gave her his rope and said with a most great and blasphemous oath that she was the bravest woman he ever saw; and so went his way without another word and troubled her no more. He and she were always good friends after that, for in her he had found a long-felt want —somebody who was not afraid of him.

THE MOTHER OF ANNE FRANK

Anne Frank, in The Diary of a Young Girl, *reveals a rare depth of understanding and compassion for a 14-year-old girl. In these two selections, she describes her growing maturity in her relationship with her mother:*

April 2, 1943:
I was lying in bed yesterday evening waiting for Daddy to come and say my prayers with me, and

wish me good night, when Mummy came into my room, sat on my bed, and asked very nicely, "Anne, Daddy can't come yet, shall I say your prayers with you tonight?" "No, Mummy," I answered.

Mummy got up, paused by my bed for a moment, and walked slowly towards the door. Suddenly she turned around, and with a distorted look on her face said, "I don't want to be cross, love cannot be forced." There were tears in her eyes as she left the room.

I lay still in bed, feeling at once that I had been horrible to push her away so rudely. But I knew too that I couldn't have answered differently. It simply wouldn't work. I felt sorry for Mummy; very, very sorry, because I had seen for the first time in my life that she minds my coldness. I saw the look of sorrow on her face when she spoke of love not being forced. It is hard to speak the truth, and yet it is the truth. . . .

January 2, 1944:

This morning when I had nothing to do I turned over some of the pages of my diary and several times I came across letters dealing with the subject "Mummy" in such a hotheaded way that I was quite shocked. . . .

I used to be furious with Mummy, and still am sometimes. It's true that she doesn't understand me, but I don't understand her either. She did love me very much and she was tender, but as she landed in so many unpleasant situations through me, and was nervous and irritable because of other worries and difficulties, it is certainly understandable that she snapped at me.

I took it much too seriously, was offended, and was rude and aggravating to Mummy, which, in turn, made her unhappy. So it was really a matter of unpleasantness and misery rebounding all the time. It wasn't nice for either of us, but it is passing.

I just didn't want to see all this, and pitied myself very much; but that, too, is understandable. Those violent outbursts on paper were only giving vent to anger which in a normal life could have been worked off by stamping my feet a couple of times in a locked room, or calling Mummy names behind her back. . . .

I soothe my conscience now with the thought that it is better for hard words to be on paper than that Mummy should carry them in her heart.

Praise your children for important things, even if you have to stretch it a bit. Praise them a lot. They live on it like bread and butter, and they need it more than bread and butter.

> —Mrs. Lavina Fugal,
> "Mother of the Year" 1955

The mother's heart is the child's schoolroom.

> —Henry Ward Beecher

You show a baby you love him a hundred times a day. You don't have to put it in words or even make an effort—in fact it's more real without the effort. It just comes through the nearness, through the hands, the tone of voice, the smiling mouth, the eyes. —Dr. Benjamin Spock

Men are what their mothers made them.

> —Ralph Waldo Emerson

When the Children Are Grown

'*THE BABY IN THE KITCHEN*'
Journalist and author Dorothy Thompson describes in her book, The Courage to Be Happy, *the visit of her two-week-old grandchild to "Grandma Dorothy's" farmhouse in New England. As she describes her feelings, it becomes evident that all the rules against pampering children went out the window the day the baby arrived—and were replaced by a grandmother's wisdom, tenderness, and love:*

As everyone, at some time during the day, gravitates toward the kitchen [of a farmhouse], so did Baby, his pretty bassinet on wheels landing plump in the middle of everything, in front of the kitchen stove, with an opened oven door, or, when it was warm and sunny, on the veranda right outside the south kitchen windows. . . .

Who took care of Baby during the day while his

mother was resting? Everybody did—whoever was nearest—and with Baby in the kitchen someone was always at hand to lay aside a duster or turn from a pot or run in from an adjoining room in response to his cries.

Was he rocked? He certainly was—a foot pushing his bassinet back and forth while its owner's hands peeled potatoes or shelled peas.

Was he always fed at exactly the prescribed hour? He was not. "He's sleeping so sweetly I wouldn't wake him up," one of Baby's numerous attendants would say. Or, "That cry means hunger, and it's clear he just didn't get enough to eat last time. Why not give him a little supplementary bottle? I've brought up too many babies to think there can be fixed rules."

Was he picked up? He certainly was, and carried and crooned to, and by everybody. . . .

When, though warm, dry, and fed, Baby cried, cramping up his legs in an obvious touch of the colic, it was the consensus of the four mothers that two drops of peppermint oil in some warm water "certainly could do him no harm"—and he quieted down.

Most of the time he slept, while the traffic milled around him, in the midst of conversation, kitchen noises, kitchen lights, and kitchen smells, or gazed up calmly at the many faces of the household, of visitors, of house guests, of children who stopped at his cradle to cluck admiringly. . . .

After five weeks, Baby and his mother had to leave, to rejoin his father in New York. The station wagon drew up at the summer-kitchen door, packed with bathinette, bassinet, chest of drawers, scales, clothes rack—what a moving! Baby in his mother's arms (he had just been fed) gazed brightly and I thought quite callously on us all.

Never kiss a baby? Everybody kissed him, in turn—on the top of his head. Grandmother Alice's eyes filled with tears; Mother Irene burst into sobs; Grandma Dorothy assumed a matter-of-fact stoicism. Secretary Ginny (who was driving them down) looked coolly efficient, but still a little nervous over her responsibility.

"Well," said [the baby's grandfather], "the mess is over. What a *happy* mess!"

"Now I must really concentrate on my work," I said—knowing that what I'd concentrate on was missing the baby.

In the kitchen the oven door of the wood range was closed. There was no rack of drying baby clothes, no bassinet, no tinkle of the Brahms cradle song.

"This kitchen seems absolutely empty," said Alice, wiping her eyes.

There were four of us in it at the time.

'MY SPECIAL GIFT'

Helen Hayes decided to write her autobiography,
On Reflection, as a legacy for her grandchildren.
In her dedication, written in the form of a letter,
she reveals the thoughts and feelings of the very
sensitive mother and grandmother behind the
legend:

My Dear Grandchildren,

At this writing, it is no longer fashionable to have
Faith; but your grandmother has never been famous for her chic, so she isn't bothered by the in-
tellectual hemlines. I have always been concerned
with the whole, not the fragments; the positive,
not the negative; the words, not the spaces between them. I loved and married my Charlie, your

grandfather, because he was both poem and poet. What wonders he could work with words.

From your parents you learn love and laughter and how to put one foot before another. But when books are opened you discover that you have wings.

No one can tell me that man's presence on earth isn't expected—even announced. Because the magi come to each new babe and offer up such treasures as to dazzle the imagination. For what are jewels and spices and caskets of gold when compared with the minds and hearts of great men?

What can a grandmother offer in the midst of such plenty? I wondered. With the feast of millennia set before you, the saga of all mankind on your bookshelf, what could I give you—Jim's children? And then I knew. Of course. My own small footnote. The homemade bread at the banquet. The private joke in the divine comedy. Your roots.

This, then, is the grandmother's special gift—a bridge to your past. . . .

Heavens knows my life hasn't always been wise and faultless. It is a pastiche made up of opposites, of lethargy and bossiness, of pride and guilt, of discipline and frivolity. It hasn't always been a model and worthy of imitation, but it was round and it was real and I lived it all greedily.

Your grandmother is an actress who has spent her working life pretending to be gay or sad, hoping that the audience felt the same. More often than not I succeeded. Offstage, I was not always in such control. The technique of living is far more elusive. Alas! One does her best and, like Thornton Wilder's Mrs. Antrobus, I have survived.

Cast by the fates as Helen Hayes, I have played the part for all it's worth. Child, maiden, sweetheart, wife, and now grandmother. We play many parts in this world and I want you to know them all—for together they make the whole. Trials and errors, hits and misses, I have enjoyed my life, children, and I pray you will, too.

This book is yours, Charlie and Mary; and I leave it in trust for you to be read only when you have reached your maturity. For this is not a fairy story but a tale of grownups who often acted like children, which is quite another thing. It is sometimes called farce and ofttimes tragedy. The combination makes the twin mask which is the symbol of the theatre in which I have spent my years.

And so—in highlights and shadows, bits and pieces, in recalled moments, mad scenes and acts of folly—all chiaroscuro and confetti—this is what it was like to be me, all the me's; what it was like to live in such exciting times and know so many of the men and women who made it so.

What are little grandchildren made of?
    Some good and some bad from Mother and Dad
    And laughs and wails and Grandmother's tales.
I love you.

                                    Grammy

'*WHERE DID THE CHILDREN GO?*'
*Pulitzer Prize-winning poet Phyllis McGinley
suddenly finds that her "girls in pinafores" are
teenagers. In this poem, "Ballade of Lost Objects,"
she echoes the universal plea of mothers: "Where
did the children vanish?"*

Where are the ribbons I tie my hair with?
    Where is my lipstick? Where are my hose—
The sheer ones hoarded these weeks to wear with
    Frocks the closets do not disclose?
Perfumes, petticoats, sports chapeaux,
    The blouse Parisian, the earring Spanish—
Everything suddenly ups and goes.
    And where in the world did the children vanish?

This is the house I used to share with
    Girls in pinafores, shier than does.
I can recall how they climbed my stair with
    Gales of giggles, on their tiptoes.
Last seen wearing both braids and bows

55

(But looking rather Raggedy-Annish),
When they departed nobody knows—
Where in the world did the children vanish?

Two tall strangers, now I must bear with,
Decked in my personal furbelows,
Raiding the larder, rending the air with
Gossip and terrible radios.
Neither my friends nor quite my foes,
Alien, beautiful, stern, and clannish,
Here they dwell, while the wonder grows:
Where in the world did the children vanish?

Prince, I warn you, under the rose,
Time is the thief you cannot banish.
These are my daughters, I suppose.
But where in the world did the children vanish?

The future destiny of the child is always the work
of the mother.   —Napoleon

Spoil your husband, but don't spoil your children
—that's my philosophy.
                                    —Mrs. Louise Currey,
                                    "Mother of the Year" 1961

'CRISES THAT
EVAPORATE OVERNIGHT'

Author Phyllis McGinley writes in Sixpence in Her Shoe *with a mother's fondness for, and insight into, her daughter's adolescence:*

I find myself hoaxed to this day by the recuperative powers of the young, even when they top me by an inch and know all about modern art. More than once I have been called long distance from a college in New England to hear news of impending disaster.

"It's exam time and I'm down with this horrible cold," croaks the sufferer, coughing dramatically. "Can you rush me that prescription of Dr. Murphy's? I don't trust our infirmary."

Envisioning flu, pneumonia, wasting fever, and a lily maid dead before her time, I harry the doctor into scribbling his famous remedy and send it by wire. Then after worrying myself into dyspepsia, I call two days later to find out the worst. An unfogged voice answers me blithely.

"What cold?" it inquires.

Ephemeral tragedies, crises that evaporate overnight are almost certain to coincide with adolescence. Gird yourselves for them. Adolescence is a disease more virulent than measles and difficult to outgrow as an allergy. At its onset parents are bewildered like the victim. They can only stand by with patience, flexibility, and plenty of food in the larder. It's amazing how consoling is a batch of cookies in an emergency. If it doesn't comfort the child, at least it helps the baker. I stopped in at a neighbor's house the other day and found her busily putting the frosting on a coconut cake.

"It's for Steven," she told me. "His pet skunk just died, and I didn't know what else to do for him."

Food helps more than understanding. Adolescence doesn't really want to be understood. It prefers to live privately in some stone tower of its own building, lonely and unassailable. To understand is to violate. This is the age—at least for girls—of hidden diaries, locked drawers, unshared secrets. It's a trying time for all concerned. The only solace is that they do outgrow it. But the flaw there is that eventually they outgrow being children too, becoming expatriates of their own tribe.

For, impossible as it seems when one first contemplates diapers and croup, then tantrums, homework, scouting, dancing class, and finally the terrible dilemmas of the teens, childhood does come inexorably to an end. Children turn into people. They speak rationally if aloofly, lecture you on manners, condescend to teach you about eclectic critism, and incline to get married. And there you

are, left with all that learning you have so pain-
fully accumulated in twenty-odd years and with
no more progeny on whom to lavish it.

Small wonder we love our grandchildren. . . .
They are our immortality. It is they who will in-
herit our wisdom, our experience, our ingenuity.

'A MOTHER'S INSIGHT'

*Hannah Lees, gifted psychologist and family coun-
selor, describes in her book* Help Your Husband
Stay Alive! *a mother's deep insight into her adolescent son's growing-up process:*

A woman I know has a son in college who loves
her tenderly but is busily rejecting her so that he
can become a man. One weekend he came home
looking awfully beat. She discovered after con-
siderably delicate probing that something important to him had not worked out the way he hoped it
would. But after telling her what was wrong in
the sketchiest sort of way he shrugged and said,
"Don't worry. I'm only being sorry for myself. I
guess I just want my mommy." She ached to comfort him but he didn't come near her or say anything more, just looked at her bleakly as if daring
her to presume on his confidence, and she knew
that, whatever he might want from mommy, he

could no longer take it from her. "The only person he could possibly have taken it from," she said with a wry smile, "was a wife. He'll find life easier in a few years when he has one."

'THE WISDOM OF EXPERIENCE'

When a mother becomes a grandmother, grown wise with the wisdom of experience, she can and often does offer inspiration for another generation. In this selection, Cameron Hawley, author of Executive Suite *and* Cash McCall, *recalls a moving incident from his own life:*

On one of the last days of my grandmother's life I sat beside her bed. Warmly reminiscent, she talked of how the world had changed during the half century since she had come to the Dakota Territory in 1878 as a pioneering bride. I asked what change she considered most significant.

Her face sobered. "I'll tell you the one I most regret," she said. "When I was a girl, there were so many men who stood out as individuals. Now there are so few.

"More and more all the time, it seems, men are yielding to some terrible compulsion to conform, to think alike and talk alike—yes, even to look alike. In those days you could recognize any man who was worth knowing as far away as you could see him or hear the sound of his voice. Believe me, no one ever mistook your grandfather for someone else. He was always his own man, thinking with his own mind, standing on his own feet. He knew that a man finds happiness only by walking his own path across the earth."

The intensity of her voice made her words an obviously purposeful warning, but years passed before I appreciated the full value of the heritage she was handing me.

Now, at fifty, looking back over my own life and the work I have done to date, I see so clearly that the things of which I am least proud have resulted from the weakness of conformity, from being more concerned with pleasing others than with satisfying myself.

My successes have come when I have had the sustained courage to follow my grandmother's admonition—in her words, to walk my own path across the earth.

Set at The Castle Press in Intertype Walbaum, a light, open typeface designed by Justus Erich Walbaum (1768-1839), who was a type founder at Goslar and at Weimar. Printed on Hallmark Eggshell Book paper. Designed by Jay D. Johnson.